DISCIPLE!
who i am & what i do

Jerry, Nancy & Robert Reed

DISCIPLE! who i am & what i do
CREED - www.creedendios.com
© 2019 CREED España with permission from Robert H. Reed
ISBN: 978-1-9164171-1-3

By Jerry, Nancy and Robert Reed
Design, layout and art by Jana Borja Taltavull

All material may be copied and shared with others.

Why the flower on the front and back cover?
This is one way to illustrate our call to be fruitful disciples of Jesus. The adventure of being a follower and disciple of Jesus is a life long adventure with significant markers along the way. It is helpful to know where the disciple! resource can fit along the journey of encouraging people to move from not knowing Christ to encountering and growing in him. The flower on the back cover includes sample resources for each stage of growth but you may want to use others. The four stages are:

1. *Seed* - **BELONG** to believe
2. *Root* - **BE** a disciple
3. *Stem* - **GROW** as a disciple
4. *Flower* - **GO** and multiply

INDEX

Introduction _____5

Preface _____9

    Step 1: Following Christ_____17
    Step 2: The Basis of Being a Disciple_____19
    Step 3: The Wheel_____21
    Step 4: The Lordship of Christ_____25
    Step 5: The Holy Spirit_____29
    Step 6: The Word_____31
    Step 7: Prayer_____33
    Step 8: Witness_____35
    Step 9: Community_____37
    Step 10: Disciple!_____39

APPENDIX

Practical helps _____41

Questions commonly asked _____43

Progress Sheets for keeping track of each encounter ___45

Study the Scriptures _____49

Prayer lists _____51

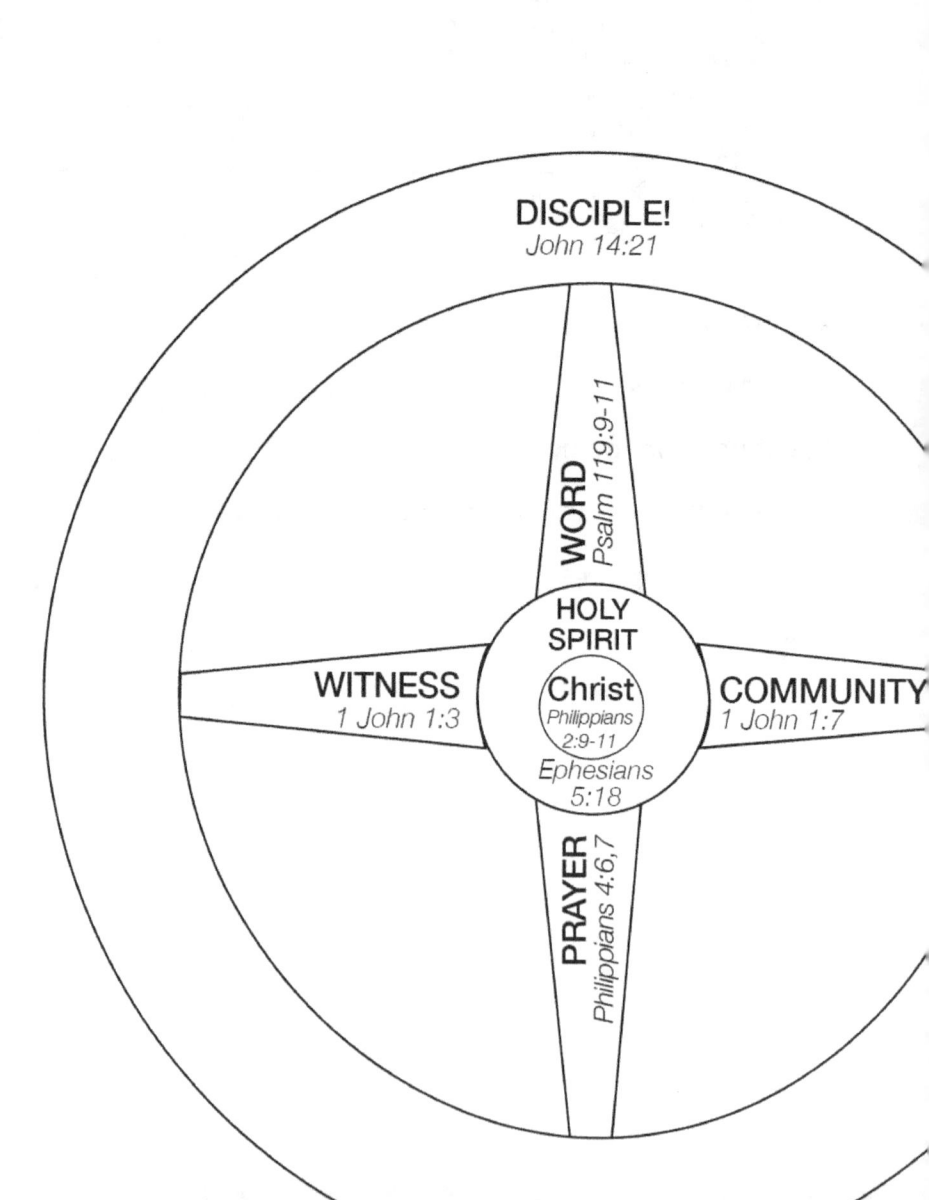

INTRODUCTION

Stop! Please don't read any further until read the **Preface** to this **DISCIPLE!** resource. The warning in the preface against the "information trap" is important background for effective discipleship. Check the boxes below as you read, and then talk about this together.

> ☐ *Please check this box when you have read the Preface on pages 9 to 15.*
>
> *Summarize in a few words what you have read:* _____
> _____
> _____
> _____
> _____
>
> *Now return to finish reading the introduction.*

Great! Thank you for reading the **Preface**. Now some considerations to help you as you proceed in the discipling process:

1. Review the **Practical Helps for Discipleship** found on pages 41 and 42. Many basic questions about discipleship are answered there.

   > ☐ *Please check this box when you have read the **Practical Helps**. Summarize in a few words what you have read:* _____
   > _____
   > _____
   > _____

2. I recommend reading in one sitting the book *Restored* by Neil T. Anderson before the *DISCIPLE!* encounters. Better yet, encourage them to go through the 10 session *Freedom in Christ Course* and the *Steps to Freedom* (freedominchrist.org). This will help them deepen their identity in Christ and discern if they are willing to deal with their "baggage" in their ongoing life-long journey as disciples and followers of Christ. The likelihood of being and reproducing fruitful disciples will greatly increase!

3. Now look at the **Progress Sheets** on pages 45 to 47. Make copies of these pages for each person in your group. Then write the name(s) of your disciple(s) in the spaces provided at the top of the page. At the close of every discipleship encounter note where you left off. Some days you may not cover the points in the material because you are dealing with other important items. Write in the date of your next encounter beside the point where you plan to begin.

☐ *Please check this box when you have made copies of the **Progress Sheets**.*

4. Remember the importance of asking a question. Questions are your friends. Use them as you disciple others. Questions allow your disciple(s) to talk and share their insights and understandings, and to ask their own questions which will often guide your conversation in unexpected but important directions.

5. As you start, agree together on the length of time you will meet together. You might suggest just two or three weeks and then decide a longer time period if you and your disciple(s) agree. An option for the first encounter with someone is to make a copy of Step One **without** the top line that says **"STEP ONE."** In this way, Step One stands alone and does not suggest that there is more to follow. Thus, it becomes easier to have early closure if you discover that the group is not working out. Be careful of "sag" in your relationship halfway through. Help those being discipled to have a sense of progress, bit by bit, as you grow together. When you end make sure you have strong closure. Do not just fade away.

6. The last consideration before you begin discipling someone is basic and easily overlooked. What are your objectives or expectations for discipling the person(s) you have in mind just now? There are different ways to answer this question.

Possible answers could include such things as having a basic understanding of what the Christian life is all about, the ability to train new Christ followers, raise up leaders among youth, leadership training for small groups, preparation for planting a new church, training people who can share pastoral responsibilities, preparing those who can teach Sunday school, and/or equipping those who might share in leading worship . One major objective in all of the above is to raise up another generation of disciples. Use your imagination to think of many more possibilities for giving sharp focus to the discipling process. Again, what is your purpose for discipling someone at this time?

Write your purpose(s) here by completing the following sentence.

My purpose at this time for getting together with [fill in the name(s) 1, 2, or 3 people here]:

_____, _____,
is to: _____
_____
_____
_____
_____

☐ *Check this box when you have written down your purpose(s).*

Remember that the nervousness you may experience as you approach those you want to disciple and grow with may come from our spiritual enemy. Satan does not want this powerful and effective process to begin. But we have victory in Jesus. Therefore pray and go, asking the Holy Spirit to fill you and use you.

PREFACE

An Ever Growing Story
There is probably nothing more satisfying than knowing that God is using you to encourage another person to grow in Christ. Many people have discovered the joy and satisfaction of helping another person grow in their Christian life using **DISCIPLE!** This preface is an adaptation of what my parents first wrote in the 1970's.

My dad discipled me. Marvin Ladner, a businessman who first discipled my dad at the university, planted a seed that continues to grow. First in Ecuador, then more significantly in Mexico, the US and around the world, the simple and yet dynamic discipling process set forth here took on a clear focus as my parents trained lay leaders to start churches and pastor them. The process continues. It began in Spanish, and then English, and now there are translations and versions in French, Japanese, Korean, Lingala, Swedish, Tagalog, Russian, Swahili, and Tenyidie (also known as Angami Naga for use in Nagaland, India). We hope to translate this revised edition into other languages as well.

As we continue to watch the dynamics of **DISCIPLE!** in many different contexts we have discovered people using the material that make up **DISCIPLE!** in different ways. The following pages are designed to help you have a positive experience in discipleship.

Discipleship - What is it?
The term discipleship in some circles has become synonymous with teaching or Christian education. The meaning of discipleship in these cases is broad and inclusive. The purpose of **DISCIPLE!** is more focused as that of an intensive relationship between an experienced person and one, two, or three others. This could also be called a mentoring relationship in which wisdom, knowledge, experience, insight, and vision is mutual as it is transferred from one to another.

Multiplication of Leaders
This form of discipleship works well in any area of church life and ministry. A woman in Mexico, using her spiritual gift of mercy, used these encounters to train other women to minister to senior women in Mexico City. In the same way, the encounters may be used by Sunday School teachers, worship leaders, church planters

or anyone with a vision for multiplying others to do what they do. In Mexico the discipleship encounters went beyond 10 generations.

Unity and Care Within the Church
While interviewing disciplers with more than twelve years of experience in Mexico City, my dad was pleasantly surprised by one woman's observation that discipleship had produced the wonderful by-product of bringing people together in the church so that they really became friends. A pastor who is a very experienced discipler, said that in his church the discipleship ministry was impacting mutual care among his members. He told of a member who had known another for sixteen years and was no more than an acquaintance. Now, because of a discipleship relationship, they are close friends and caring for one another.

More Than One-on-One
People mistakenly speak of this dynamic discipling process as a one-on-one discipleship approach. While it is true that often we do have one-on-one discipleship encounters, this must be seen as an accommodation to a better approach. Ideally two or three disciples in a group provide the best dynamic for discipleship. When there are two or three together being part of the Body of Christ is more easily experienced. Body life can more easily be learned in this context. There is also an implicit kind of accountability present when there is more than just one disciple when you get together.

Discipling or Teaching? Encounters or Classes?
A special note to those who might use this material — before you start to "disciple" people you need to make a decision. The decision is one of focus. Do you plan to teach the content of **DISCIPLE!** or are you going to invest in relationships to help grow character, the fruit of the Spirit, and see multiplication take place?

If your focus is on teaching the content of this material I would strongly urge you to do so **without calling the process discipleship.** Discipleship is much more than just teaching information. If you are looking for a title to use in the case of teaching this material you could call it "Training in Christian Basics." In this case, you will have "classes" and not "encounters" when you meet. An "encounter" is the meeting together of you, and your disciple(s), with the Lord for growth through prayer, and a community that encourages, as well as the study of the Bible in the context of daily living.

Formation or Information?

It is this dynamic approach to discipleship that is encouraged with these encounters. The focus is on Christ followers growing into the likeness of Jesus Christ. The intent is the formation of a godly life and character along with a basic knowledge of the Bible. By way of comparison, in the classroom context, knowledge or **information** is the focus, while in the discipling context, **formation**, i.e. character, principles, values, vision, and goals, (along with knowledge) becomes the focus. On the one hand, the teaching approach tells us that Jesus is Lord. On the other hand the discipleship approach helps us to experience the Lordship of Jesus in our daily lives.

With this discipleship model, life is shared with others. There is growth together. Vision and ministry are both shared and taught. Dependency on the Lord Jesus increases as we bear fruit. Thus discipleship can involve nurture, evangelism, church planting, prayer, worship, and justice and peace issues all at the same time.

The Ideal Context For Vision Casting

Leaders must have a vision -- a mental picture of what tomorrow will look like. They see a future in ministry and its exciting possibilities. However, most vision casters have found that their followers (disciples) will probably forget the vision within a month unless that vision is repeated over and over in different ways. The vision of a church I pastored was **"Overflow with Jesus to make more disciples in a more just and caring world."** We need to be reminded again and again of our core identity and purpose as ministers of reconciliation empowered by the Spirit of Christ to make fruitful disciples that transform society. The **DISCIPLE!** encounters provide a context for casting a vision and reinforcing it over a period of many months.

One Life Impacting Another Life

An illustration may help to show the dynamics of one person impacting another through the discipling process. As little Maria approached her old doll house on the back porch she remembered how her Daddy had transformed the looks of the garage door earlier in the day. He had taken a can off the garage shelf, opened it, added some water, stirred and began painting. So Maria decided she would paint her doll house. She found a can, added water, stirred and with a small brush from the garage began painting one end of the doll house. When one end was finished she stood back to see how nice it looked. To her surprise it looked the same. Nothing had happened! When her Daddy came to see what the problem was he discovered that she was painting with water.

Maria had gone through the motions of mixing and painting but there was no change in the final product. She lacked just one thing -- the pigment, the color. And so it is with discipleship. Simply using the encounters as material for teaching is the same as painting with water. For true discipleship to take place we need to share the pigment of our lives. Pigment represents our seeking the fullness of the Holy Spirit but also such things as our passion, our vision, our hunger for more of God, our feeling weak and casting ourselves in dependence upon the Lord, our honesty, our search for purity -- all of this and more. These are more easily caught than taught. That is why we say that the **DISCIPLE!** encounters are a pretext for meeting together.

Time and Multiplication

The fruit of discipleship is seen after you have invested time in a relationship and let the pigment of your life impact the life of your disciples (as you depend on being filled with the Holy Spirit). There are no short cuts. This is more than a ten-week process. Six months to two years is realistic. I find that nine months is usually adequate for a discipleship relationship to bear fruit. By the time the disciples have come to step five in the process they should be selecting the people they will be meeting with on a regular basis for their own discipleship encounters.

This means that you will still be available week after week to encourage and help your disciples to have a positive and lasting impact on the next generation of disciples. Ideally, by the time you have finished step ten and some experiences of going deeper together in "Study the Scriptures" (p. 45), your disciples should be doing well in their own **DISCIPLE!** encounters and you can begin again with another small group of two or three people.

I have also had failures in discipleship. Sometimes early in the process and other times later, someone drops out. I have worked with those who never reproduced themselves. These cases throw me back on the Lord in dependence and weakness. Yet the successes far outweigh the failures. Discipleship is worth the risk of some failure along the way. We are always learning.

This Preface should serve as a guideline and not a hard and fast rule. But there is one rule of thumb that should continually be applied in the discipling process: Is what I am teaching, showing, and demonstrating easily transferable and "pass-on-able?" We hear many good sermons, and there are many good seminars and classes available which help build up our knowledge, but most are not designed to be easily transmitted to others. **Keep it simple!**

A Pretext for Meeting Together

Since the discipling process depends on the dynamic factors mentioned above, we make every effort to avoid the subtle traps that could make it just another class or time consuming effort. Thus the ***DISCIPLE!*** encounters become the pretext for meeting and growing together. All the people involved in the process grow together. We offer a list of practical helps on pages 41 and 42 that will answer the most commonly asked questions and provide guidelines for those who are just getting started.

Whom Shall I Disciple?

The question always comes up, "Whom shall I disciple?"
These include:

1. **New Christ followers.** Initially *DISCIPLE!* was written for new believers so that they could immediately share their new found faith in Jesus Christ with their family members and friends. Basic to the process was the vision that these new Christ followers would soon begin to disciple their own friends and relatives as soon as they came to know Christ.

2. **Fervent Christ followers.** Without a clear sense of direction and purpose, younger fervent Christ followers easily lose the freshness in their walk with Jesus. The ***DISCIPLE!*** resource provides the context and focus for continued growth and purposeful ministry..

3. **Vintage Christ followers.** The ***DISCIPLE*!** encounters provide the framework to help seasoned Christ followers organize their knowledge so that they can pass it on to others -- especially to those new Christ followers that they are praying for. Also the encounters provide the very exciting possibility for renewal among those who desire more of God in their lives. In discipleship we grow together - both the disciples and the discipler.

4. **Pre-Christ followers.** Resources like *Christianity Explored, Alpha* (alpha.org) and the Alpha booklet *Why Jesus?*, could be used to meet and invite people into a relationship with Christ before using **DISCIPLE!** or as a part of Step One.

5. **Your own children.** My dad took each of his teenage children out for breakfast once a week before school as a wonderful time to "check in" with us. We inched our way through the encounters as we talked about school, friends, etc. Having our best friends join us worked out especially well. My dad started with me when I was in primary school - once a week after school for ice cream. In this case we suggest an abbreviated, more easy going approach using the graphics to help communicate the basics. For children from reading age through about age twelve I encourage you to use Daphne Kirk's encounters series called "Living with Jesus." They can be found at www.gnation2gnation.com.

Acknowledgments

The discipler will readily discern that these encounters contain little that is original. My parents, Jerry and Nancy Reed, compiled the initial outlines for these encounters in Ecuador, South America. They used the Navigator's Wheel Illustration to determine the major themes of the material. Many disciples, disciplers and ministry peers helped in the development of this tool. Later, following the adaptation suggested by some friends, the Hub was added to represent the Holy Spirit.

After returning to the United States, my dad taught evangelism, discipleship, and church growth at North Park Theological Seminary in Chicago. For several years my mom worked directly with national church leaders in Latin America, Spain, and the Hispanic church in the U.S.A.

My dad passed away in the Spring of 2011. God used that season of grief to remind me of my primary identity and vocation. I am a loved one, I am a holy one, and a saint. I am secure, accepted and significant in Christ. I am called. **DISCIPLE!** This is both a noun and verb - it is my identity and call. I am a disciple of Jesus called to make disciples.

Marv Ladner, the man who spent time discipling my dad during his college years told him: "Jerry, don´t forget that when everything is said and done – when you are at the end of your ministry and life, it will be the time invested in the lives of people that really counts. When the dust settles and there is no more activity, it will be transformed lives, people that live for the Lord, that will make all the difference."

As a part of the legacy I have received from my parents, I pass on this tool to help the body of Christ disciple as identity and call. ***DISCIPLE! who I am & what I do.***

Robert Reed
2020

STEP 1 — *FOLLOWING CHRIST*

1. **Talk about what you believe and why.** If someone were to ask you who a Christ follower is, what would you say? Who and what do you believe in and why?

2. **READ, DISCOVER & DISCUSS** – *"Holy Spirit come among us as we read, discuss and apply your Word."*

   What is salvation? What are we saved from? (See 1 Peter 1:18) What are we saved for? How are we saved?

   Read and discuss passages from Scripture including the ones below. In this step and all of the rest feel free to read all, some, and/or find other Scripture texts.

   - Genesis 3, John 3 *(compare)*
   - Romans 10
   - Revelation 3:14-22
   - Ephesians 2:8-22

   In this and every Step feel free to share other biblical texts you discover.
   What have you been saved from and for? See 1 Peter 1:18 (Avoid "church" and "religious" language)

3. **The Four Assurances**

   Satan especially attacks new Christ followers in these four areas. We defend ourselves with the Word of God even as Jesus did. – *Matthew 4:4,7,10*

   3.1 ☐ The assurance of salvation
   1 John 5:11,12

   3.2 ☐ The assurance of victory over temptation
   1 Corinthians 10:13

   3.3 ☐ The assurance of forgiveness
   1 John 1:9

3.4 ☐ The assurance of God's provision for our needs
John 16:24

Booklets such as the Alpha "Why Jesus?" help us explain to others how to know and follow with Jesus. Google and watch the Alpha film series video "Who is Jesus?".

TO DO:

☐ *Google search and watch the Alpha* film series video "Who is Jesus?"*

☐ *Memorize** Revelation 3:20 and* ☐ *Romans 10:9. Consider memorizing the four assurances.*

Notes:
*If you go to www.alpha.org and register you can download this video and others for the following week.

**To memorize write down the verses on cards to have them on hand to review or try http://www.remem.me/

STEP 2 – *THE BASIS OF BEING A DISCIPLE*

Romans 1:11,12 *"For I want very much to see you, in order to share a spiritual blessing with you to make you strong. What I mean is, that both you and I will be helped at the same time, you by my faith and I by yours."* Good News Bible

1. Making disciples

1.1 The illustration of the two seas:

A. The Dead Sea — does not support life because it doesn't allow water to go in and flow out. *(Christ followers who just receive and don't share the gospel and the Christian life with others.)*

B. The Sea of Galilee — supports life because water comes in and goes out *(Christ followers who share Christ with others.)*

1.2 Four Generations

A. Four generations — a biblical model of multiplying disciples. The gospel and the Christian life are shared simply with others so that they can easily be passed on from the first to the fourth generation and beyond.

2 Timothy 2:2
- 1st generation – Paul
- 2nd generation – Timothy
- 3rd generation – Faithful people
- 4th generation – Others

B. Four generation principle in the Old Testament
 - Psalm 78:5,6; Joel 1:3

2. READ, DISCOVER & DISCUSS – *"Holy Spirit come among us as we read, discuss and apply what you teach us."*

- Mark 3
- John 15
- 2 Timothy 2

What is a disciple? How did Jesus call and train his disciples? How about the apostle Paul?

What are some characteristics of a disciple?

In this and every Step feel free to share other biblical texts you discover.

3. Information verses formation.

Look at the description and percentages of the diagram below.. Do you agree? Why or why not?

- Information *(10% of the discipleship effort)*
- Formation *(90% of the discipleship effort)*

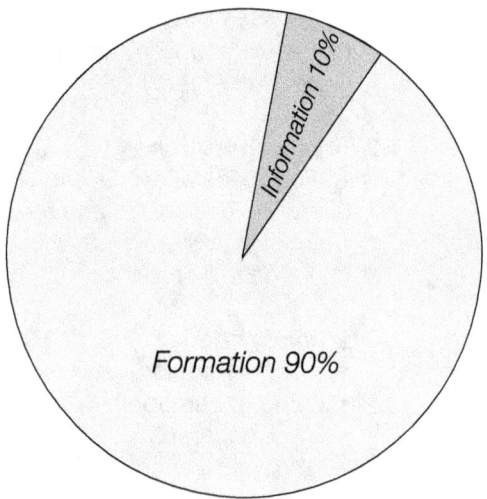

If we put a percentage to how Jesus trained his disciples, about 90% was formation and 10% was information. Formation has to do with shaping identity and character development with the fruit of the Spirit of love, joy, peace, patience, goodness, kindness, faithfulness, gentleness and self-control. *(Galatians 5:22-23).* Transferring information takes relatively little time. The formation of character and identity takes a lifetime.

4. What are the requirements of discipleship found in *Luke 14:25-33*? *(This is a familiar Hebraic form of teaching using extreme contrasts.)*

5. Find at least ten privileges of discipleship in John 15:7-16.

1. _____
2. _____
3. _____
4. _____
5. _____
6. _____
7. _____
8. _____
9. _____
10. _____

6. The discipleship relationship — Spiritual authority comes as a result of working with and voluntarily under others.

> *Notice how Titus is commissioned by Paul — Titus 1:5 — to act with authority — Titus 2:15.*
>
> *Also observe how Paul is subject to the Apostles — Acts 15:1,2; 16:4.and Galatians 2:9,10. We recognize and submit to spiritual authority. It is not imposed.*

TO DO

☐ *Memorize 2 Timothy 2:2*

☐ *Memorize Ephesians 2:8-10*

☐ *Read all of Ephesians*

STEP 3 — *THE WHEEL*

1.1. Set aside a routine time alone in relationship with God.

• *Talk about Christ's example— Mark 1:32-35 (Talk about your example and experience.)*

• *Begin with 7-10 minutes a day to pray, read the Word. The morning prayer of the Celtic Daily Prayer can be helpful (northumbriacommunity.org/offices/morning-prayer/)*

Needed: a time, a place, a plan a Bible, and a journal

2. READ, DISCOVER & DISCUSS – *"Holy Spirit come among us as we read, discuss and apply what you teach us."*

Ephesians - *note how Paul organized Ephesians and his other letters in two parts. There is no command as in "do this" in the first half of Ephesians. Chapters 1-3 can be described as BEING (identity and benefits) and chapters 4-6 as DOING (pastoral advice).*

How would you describe these two parts? Why did Paul write this way? Why is this important for us?

3. The Wheel* – (Shows the relationship of the themes of each STEP that follows in these **DISCIPLE!** encounters.

- **Christ** — The Axle, the center of life *(Philippians 2:9-11)*
- **Holy Spirit** — The Hub *(Ephesians 5:18)*
- The VERTICAL SPOKES *(God speaks to us through his Word and we speak with God through prayer*
  - **Word** — *Psalm 119:9-11; Matthew 4:4*
  - **Prayer** — *Philippians 4:6,7; John 15:7*

- The HORIZONTAL SPOKES *(We reach out to Christ followers in fellowship and to non-Christ followers through our witness).*
  - **Community** — *I John 1:7*
  - **Witness** — *I John 1:3*

• THE DISCIPLE LIVING IN AND FOR CHRIST — John 14:21; John 15:5 - the wheel holds everything together.

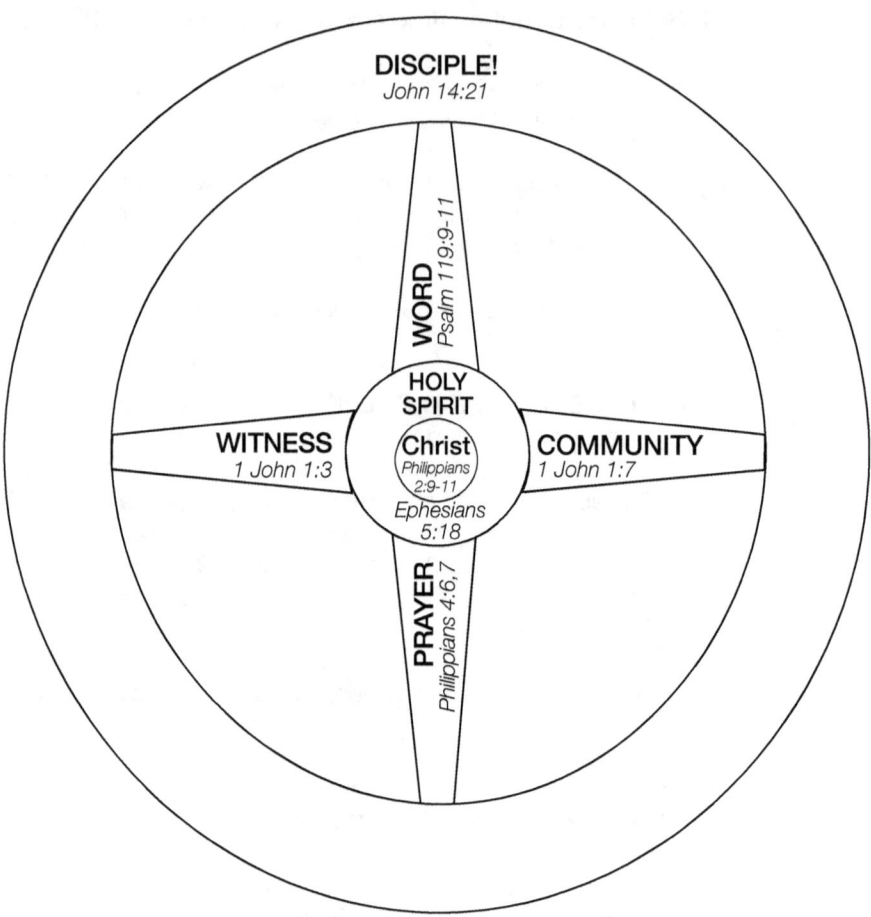

TO DO

☐ *Memorize John 15:5 and the parts of the wheel.*

☐ *Time alone with God. Begin with 7-10 minutes a day. Read Philippians.*

☐ *Google search and watch the Alpha Film Series talk "How can I have faith?"*

*Adapted from the Navigators' Wheel Illustration

STEP 4 – *THE LORDSHIP OF CHRIST*

1. The Bible speaks of Jesus as Lord.*
The definition of the word Lord is: owner, chief, governor, slave owner, highest authority, king. This word indicates: position, complete control, greatest authority, master.
How do you respond to the question posed in Luke 6:46?

2. READ, DISCOVER & DISCUSS – *"Holy Spirit come among us as we read, discuss and apply what you teach us."*

- *Luke 6*
- *Philippians (focus on chapter 2)*

In Philippians 2 what can we learn from the example of Jesus? What does it mean that Jesus is Lord ad that "every knee shall bow, every tongue confess that Jesus Christ is Lord…"?

3. Choose 2 or 3 areas you struggle with to live under the new management of Jesus as Lord of your life.
    3.1 Priorities-Matthew 6:33
    3.2 Things-clothing, cars, etc. Luke 12:15
    3.3 Social standing-Matthew 20:26-28
    3.4 Power- 1 Peter 5:5,6
    3.5 Pride-Romans 12:3
    3.6 Family-Luke 14:26; Matthew 10:37
    3.7 Escapism-drugs, alcohol, Ephesians. 5:18
    3.8 Pleasure-Mark 4:19
    3.9 Egoism-Philippians 2:3,4
    3.10 Money-Ecclesiastes 5:10,11; Psalm 62:10
    3.11 Sex-1 Corinthians 6:18-20; Matthew 5:27-28
    3.12 Anxiety-Romans 8:28; Philippians 4:63.13
    3.13 Good deeds-Romans 4:4,5; Ephesians. 2:8-10
    3.14 Tithe-Malachi 3:8-10; 2 Corinthians 8:1-8, 9:6-8
    3.15 Fear-2 Timothy 1:7; 1 John 4:4,18
    3.16 Thought life-Philippians 4:8; Colossians 3:2
    3.17 Critical spirit-Matthew 7:1-3
    3.18 Bitterness-Hebrews 12:14,15

3.19 The tongue-James 3:2; Proverbs 26:20-22
3.20 Envy-Proverbs 14:30; 1 Peter 2:1
3.21 Bad temper-Proverbs 16:32; 2 Timothy 1:7
3.22 Irresponsibility-1 Corinthians 4:2; Matthew 25:14-30
3.23 Care of the body-1 Corinthians 6:19,20
3.24 Lying-Lev 19:11; Ephesians 4:25
3.25 Resentment-Proverbs 10:12; 1 Peter 3:9
3.26 Forgiveness-Mark 11:25
3.27 Other (racism, prejudice, deceit, cheating, etc.)

*In the New Testament, the word Savior occurs only 24 times and the word Lord occurs over 600 times, thus showing the importance of Jesus' Lordship.

4. Read — *Romans 12:1,2. What does it mean for Jesus to be on the throne of your life?*

Who sits on the throne of your life?

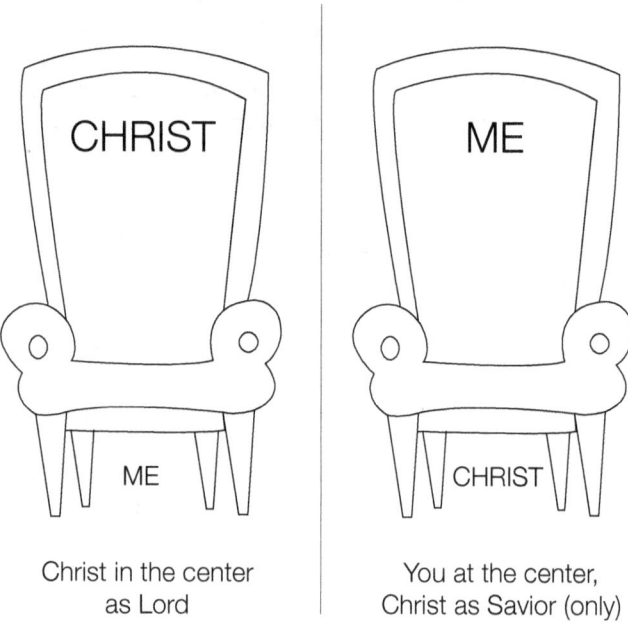

Christ in the center as Lord | You at the center, Christ as Savior (only)

Consider the idea of giving over all your rights to God. With God as your defender, there is no reason to feel offended or a victim. of injustice. .

Consider the idea of giving everything you have over to God — Genesis 22:1-18

- *What did Abraham offer to God?*
- *What did God do with this sacrifice?*
- *Can you trust God to do what is best with your life and possessions if you give them to Him?*

TO DO

☐ Memorize Philippians 2:9-11

☐ Choose one of the areas of struggle to develop a Stronghold-buster*. Identify the lie behind the struggle. Find 4-5 verses that state the truth in this area. Write a statement to RENOUNCE the lie and DECLARE the truth. Read it in faith for 40 days. Repeat with the next area. Share your stronghold buster next week.

☐ Read Acts 1 and 2.

☐ Google search and watch the two Alpha Film Series talks "Who is the Holy Spirit?" and "What does the Holy Spirit do?"

*For help with "Stronghold-busting" search on the web: "rightnowmedia.org - Freedom in Christ - Renewing the Mind -Session 9 - Renewing the Mind "

---

*This illustration of Christ or Self being on the Throne of your life is adapted from the booklet by CRU (before Campus Crusade for Christ), Inc. 1966.

STEP 5 – *THE HOLY SPIRIT*

1. Every believer has the Holy Spirit
    1.1 Sealed with the Holy Spirit — Ephesians 1:13
    1.2 The Holy Spirit gives testimony to our spirit — Rm. 8:16

2. READ, DISCOVER & DISCUSS – *"Holy Spirit come among us as we read, discuss and apply what you teach us."*
- *Acts 2*
- *Galatians 5*
- *John 14:15-31*

Who is the Holy Spirit?
What are some symbols of the Holy Spirit?
What does the Holy Spirit do?
What are the gifts of the Spirit?
What is the fruit of the Spirit?
How have you experienced being filled with the Holy Spirit?

3. The Bible speaks of being filled with the Spirit – Acts 1:8; Ephesians 5:18. There are a variety of experiences. *(Acts 2:1-4; 8:14-17; 9:17-18; 10:44-48; 19:1-6)*

Compare Acts 2:1-4 with Acts 4:31 - a continuous experience of being filled with the Holy Spirit again and again.

4. We are involved in a spiritual conflict
(2 Corinthians 10:3-5):
    4.1 Against the world –*1 John 2:15-21, John 16:33*
    4.2 Against the flesh *(human nature)*
       – *Galatians 5:16-17; Romans 8:9,13*
    4.3 Against the devil –*1 Peter 5:7-9; Ephesians. 6:10 -13*
    4.4 We are given armor to defend ourselves – *Ephesians 5*

After listing all of the armor, Paul says, "Pray in the Spirit at all times…" What does that mean? How can we do this?

TO DO

☐ *Memorize Ephesians 5:18 - We are told to "Be filled with the Holy Spirit."*

☐ *Google search and watch the Alpha Film Series talk, "How can I be filled with the Spirit?"*

☐ *Plan some time together to read and put into practice this truth. Consider an evening together for dinner. Pray to be filled with the Holy Spirit!*

STEP 6 – THE WORD

1. Why do we use the Bible as our basis for the Christian life? — *2 Timothy 3:16,17; 2 Peter 1:20,21*

2. READ, DISCOVER & DISCUSS – *"Holy Spirit come among us as we read, discuss and apply what you teach us."*
- *Psalm 119* — This Psalm, the longest in the Bible, was organized in such a way to be memorized. Each section begins with a letter of the Hebrew alphabet.
- *Matthew 4:1-11*
- *Hebrews 4:12-16*
- *2 Timothy 3:10-17*

3. Five ways of growing in the Word of God to then apply to our daily living*:

TO DO
☐ *Memorize the names of the Books of the Bible*

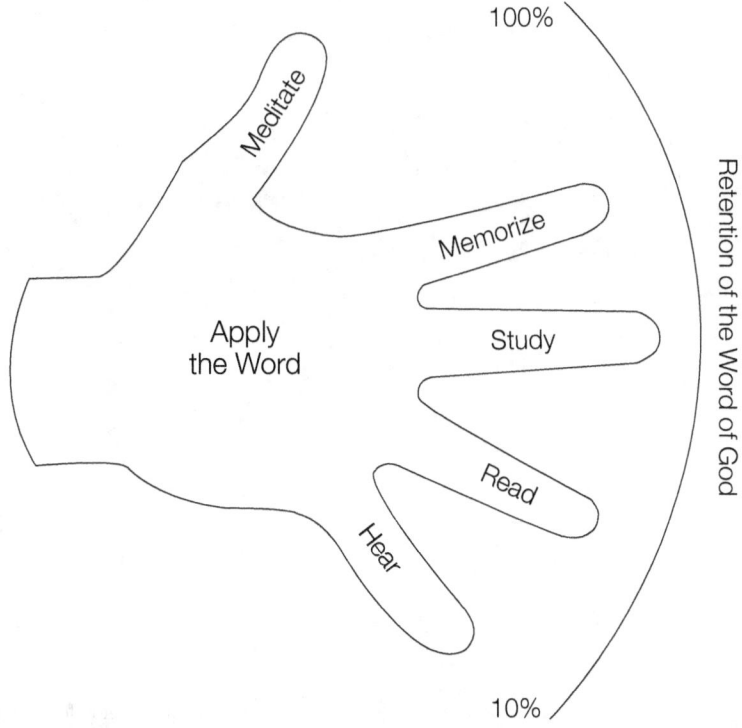

☐ *Memorize Psalm 119:9-11*

☐ *Memorize the Hand Illustration*

☐ *Google & watch the Alpha Film Series talk "Why & how should I read the Bible?"*

*Illustration adapted from "The Navigators"

STEP 7 — *PRAYER*

Prayer is talking with God, a two-way conversation opening up to Him, and listening to Him. You can pray anywhere at any time.

1. Elements of prayer in the Lord's Prayer *(Matthew 6)*
— Prayer "FACTS":
- **F**amily — *children, intimate relationship* – "Our Father…"
- **A**dore — "Holy is your name…"
- **C**onfess — "Forgive us our sins as we forgive…"
- **T**hanks — forgiveness, provision *(daily bread)*, protection…
- **S**upplication — "Your Kingdom come… Give us… Deliver us from evil…" - requests for yourself and for others

2. READ, DISCOVER & DISCUSS — *"Holy Spirit come among us as we read, discuss and apply what you teach us."*
- Matthew 6:5-34
- John 17
- Psalm 88
- Ephesians 1:15-23; Ephesians 6:10-20

What can hinder our prayers?

3. Practices of prayer
- 3.1 Centering Prayer *(www.centeringprayer.com)*
- 3.2 The Prayer of Examen *(www.ignatianspirituality.com)*
- 3.3 Other types of Prayer

4. Collective or corporate prayer
— Acts 2:42; 4:31; Mathew. 18:19-20; 2 Chronicles 7:14

TO DO

☐ *Memorize Philippians 4:6,7*

☐ *Develop a way to pray for others regularly (perhaps a daily list).*

☐ *Google search & watch the Alpha film series "Why and how should I pray?"*

☐ *Begin reading the Psalms, as well as hymns and choruses, and make a list of the various names and descriptions of God for use in praise and prayer.*

☐ *Connect the verse with the description:*

A. 1 John 5:14,15

B. 2 Corinthians 12:7-9

C. John 11:1-44

D. Acts 3:1-10

E. Deuteronomy 7:22

1. Delayed answer "wait"

2. Different answer

3. Definite answer "yes"

4. Step by step answer

5. Denied answer "no"

STEP 8 — *WITNESS*

1. Ways of witnessing
    1.1 Your life — James 1:22
    "What you are speaks so loudly I can't hear what you say." Emerson

    1.2 Your words — 1 John 1:3; 1 Peter 3:15
        A. Direct evangelism — 2 Timothy 1:8
        B. Indirect evangelism — share your own experience of God's power in your life.

    1.3 Your concerned prayer for a friend's need or problem - Acts 28:8

2. READ, DISCOVER & DISCUSS – *"Holy Spirit come among us as we read, discuss and apply what you teach us."*
- *John 3*
- *Acts 8:26-40*
- *2 Corinthians 5:11-21*
- *Ephesians 2*

3. What is your story of faith in Christ? *(1 John 1:1-3)*
Paul's story--Acts 26:4-23; 22:1-21. His story can be divided into three parts:

    A. **B.C** — How life was Before knowing Christ
    — Acts 26:4-11
    B. **M.C** — The Moment he came to know Christ
    — Acts 26:12-18
    C. **A.C** — How life has been After knowing Christ
    — Acts 26:19-23

4. MISSIONAL witness
    4.1 *"Martyria"* – Translated as "witness." We are called to give our lives in love for Christ and others. This is what it means to be a witness ("martyria" is where we get the word "martyr").
    4.2 Do justice, love mercy and walk humbly with your God — Micah 6:84

4.3 Witness (*Greek=martyria*) + Service (*Greek=diakonia*) + Community (*Greek=koinonis*) + Evangelism (*Greek=euangelion*) + Worship (*Greek=liturgia*)

> Note to 4.3:
> This is the overall order we observe in the first part of the book of Acts. We give of ourselves (witness) in love (service) to form relationships of trust (community) so people can know the good news of Christ and his forgiveness (evangelism) and then join (worship) with us.
>
> *What do you think about this order?*

5. The scope of our witness is seen in Jesus' last words known as the Great Commission
- Matthew. 28:19-20 - the importance of these can be seen when we compare them to the first words he spoke to his disciples —
- Matthew. 4:19 - remember his command to pray.
- Mt. 9:37-38 - this witness starts at home and extends outward
- Acts 1:8 - in ever larger circles to include the whole world —

TO DO

☐ *Memorize 1 John 1:3*

☐ *Memorize Micah 6:8*

☐ *Go to the web page www.transformourworld.org and talk about it next week.*

☐ *Write your own story of faith in Christ, using the three parts mentioned in Section 3 of this step. It may be your M.C. (Moment you came to know Christ) was more or a process than one moment you can remember. Be ready to share the next time we meet.*

☐ *Share your story with someone. It is good to have a three-minute version and others that are longer.*

☐ *Google and watch the Alpha film series "Why and how should I tell others?"*

STEP 9 — COMMUNITY

1. Community is unity among the members of a group. It has to do with companionship, friendly association, a mutual sharing of an experience, activity or interest. Community in a Christian context is one family living together under one leader, Christ. We all follow Him while we love one another, help one another, and learn from one another. The early church met in homes. Look at the last chapter of Romans and other of Paul's epistles where he greets "the church that meets in the home of…"

2. READ, DISCOVER & DISCUSS – *"Holy Spirit come among us as we read, discuss and apply what you teach us."*
- *1 John 1*
- *Romans 12*
- *Acts 2:42-47*

3. One definition of a small group Christ-like community is:
"A group of 3-15 people (any age) who meet weekly outside the church building to experience the love and power of Jesus with the goal of making disciples that make disciples which results in the multiplication of the group and the transformation of people."

Talk about this definition:
What do you like?
What is challenging?
Where do you find these principles in the Bible?
Are you doing this?

TO DO
- ☐ *Memorize 1 John 1:7*
- ☐ *Google search and watch the Alpha film series "What about the church?"*
- ☐ *Read "Ekklesia" by Edgardo Silvoso*

STEP 10 — DISCIPLE!

Note: The word "disciple" is both a noun and a verb - it is who we are and what we do. Talk about this.

1. What is the goal of life? *(Colossians 1:28; John 15:5; Ephesians 5:10)*

2. READ, DISCOVER & DISCUSS – "Holy Spirit come among us as we read, discuss and apply what you teach us."
- *John 14 & 15*
- *Hebrews 12:1-14*
- *Matthew 28*
- *The book Ekklesia*

What does it mean to disciple people and nations? What is the next step God is calling you to take?

3. Some things God promises those who obey Him
    3.1 Blessings – *Deuteronomy 28:1-14; Joshua 1:8*
    3.2 Persecution and suffering – *2 Tim. 3:12; 1 Peter 4:12-16*
    3.3 Being a friend of God – *John 15:14*
    3.4 Being loved by God – *John 14:21*

TO DO

☐ *Memorize John 14:21*

☐ *If you have not done so yet, pray and plan who you will disciple*

☐ *Google search and watch the Alpha film series "How can I make the most of the rest of my life?"*

PRACTICAL HELPS FOR DISCIPLESHIP

1. Start by agreeing to meet with your potential disciple(s) for only two to four weeks. After that, if mutually agreed upon, you are free to continue.

2. Decide where you will start - Step One or by using Alpha *(alpha.org)* or reading the book "Restored" by Neil T. Anderson.

3. Begin each weekly encounter with prayer.

4. Have the materials on hand (outlines — lessons, cards for verses, etc.)

5. In general, go to meet them rather than wait for them to come to you. If there are several disciples, choose the home or choice of place of the one who would have the most difficulty in coming.

6. Consider giving out the outlines step by step — a page at a time for the first two steps.

7. Have a system for notifying if someone is not able to attend.

8. Meet around a table for ease in writing and using the Bible.

9. Use an hour to an hour and a half of time.

10. Share group leadership. Let others talk.

11. Women meet with women and men with men.

12. If there are two or more persons in the group and one misses an encounter, have one of the others in the group catch them up.

13. Don't take anything for granted. That is why the outlines begin with what it means to know and follow Christ. That is why we memorize Revelation 3:20.

14. Don't try to force an issue; allow the Holy Spirit to act.

15. Pace yourself and the group. It is not necessary to read all the biblical passages listed. Need and time must be taken into account. Take time to allow the person(s) to understand the content, not only the theoretical parts, but also their practical applications to life.

16. Develop a personal relationship, not just as student to teacher, but as friends. Plan to do some social activities together.

17. Talk about problems as they come up. Pray with your disciple(s) and direct them towards a practical solution. If there are critical problems at the moment, first handle them and then continue with the encounter. Don't hesitate to ask for help from a Christ follower whom you respect.

18. Share openly with them your own spiritual needs and personal problems (we all have them).

19. Review the outlines once in awhile. Have the disciple present or review the outlines with you or better yet, with someone else.

20. Remember that "information" is necessary, but the goal is "formation" of disciples for the Lord.

21. Time with the disciples may include:
    21.1 Check-in – How are you? (You share first)
    21.2 Check-up (To do, memorization, etc.)
    21.3 Handle problems as they arise.
    21.4 Prayer
    21.5 Continue with the encounter.

22. Have the disciples in the group write the memory verse on their cards before they leave.

23. Before ending plan for the next one by making notes on the Progress Sheet or on your own "lesson plan."

24. Remember, being involved in ministry gives a sense of direction to everyone involved in discipleship. Share life and ministry experiences not just "meetings."

25. Never allow your discipling relationships to just fizzle out. Always have closure. Celebrate what has been accomplished.

QUESTIONS COMMONLY ASKED ABOUT DISCIPLESHIP

Question. *Am I doing it right? After four months, I'm only on Step #4. It seems like we spend so much time talking about "other things."*

Answer. You are right on target. There is no given time frame. Many people will take a year. Some more time and others less. You would not touch on the "other things" if you did not have the outlines in front of you as your "pretext" for getting together. You are all growing!

Question. *Now that we are discipling people in the church, should we organize a committee to keep it going?*

Answer. Discipleship depends on vision and relationships. Selecting a promoter to encourage people and to organize an annual banquet or semi-annual half-day retreat and to lift up the discipleship vision is a good idea. Periodic words of encouragement in the weekly bulletin are always appropriate and help create an ongoing interest in discipleship for the whole church. This requires little organization.

PROGRESS SHEET

Make copies of these Progress Sheets as needed.

For the discipler
> The ☐☐ *indicates homework. Check off the first ☐ when an assignment is given and the second ☐ when it is completed.*

Name of disciple(s):

1. _____
2. _____
3. _____
4. _____

STEP 1 – *Following Christ* *(Mark first ☐ assigned. Mark second ☐ completed)*

TO DO
(Page 18)
☐☐ *Revelation 3:20*   ☐☐ *1 John.5:11-12*
☐☐ *Romans 10:9*   ☐☐ *1 Corinthians 10:13*
☐☐ *Alpha Video*   ☐☐ *1 John.1:9*
                       ☐☐ *John 16:24*

STEP 2 – *The Basis of Being a Disciple*

TO DO
(Page 20)
☐☐ *2 Timothy 2:2*   ☐☐ *Ephesians 2:8-10*
☐☐ *Read all of Ephesians*

STEP 3 – *The Wheel*
TO DO
(Page 22)
☐☐ *John 15:5 & the Wheel*   ☐☐ *Read all of Philippians*
☐☐ *Time alone with God*   ☐☐ *Alpha video*

STEP 4 - *The Lordship of Christ*
Is your disciple praying for others to disciple?

TO DO
(Page 25)
- ☐☐ Philippians 2:9-11 ☐☐ Read Acts 1 & 2
- ☐☐ Stronghold buster ☐☐ Alpha video

STEP 5 – *The Holy Spirit*

TO DO
(Page 26)
- ☐☐ *Ephesians 5:18*
- ☐☐ *Alpha video*
- ☐☐ *Plan and spend time together to pray to be filled with the Holy Spirit*

List the names of those your disciple(s) want to disciple:

_____
_____
_____
_____

STEP 6 – *The Word*
Are your disciples discipling yet?
Encourage them.

TO DO
(Page 30)
- ☐☐ *Books of the Bible* ☐☐ *Hand Illustration*
- ☐☐ *Psalm 119:9-11* ☐☐ *Alpha video*

STEP 7 - *Prayer*
Talk about who those in your group are discipling. Suggest all getting together to meet and pray sometime.

TO DO
(Page 32)
- ☐☐ *Philippians 4:6,7*
- ☐☐ *Alpha video*
- ☐☐ *List of descriptions of God*

☐☐ *Plan to pray for others* _____
_____
_____
_____
_____

☐☐ *Complete chart*

STEP 8 – *Witness*
Encourage each disciple in their efforts to disciple others.

TO DO
(Page 34)
- ☐☐ *1 John 1:3* ☐☐ *Write your personal story*
- ☐☐ *Micah 6:8* ☐☐ *Share your story*
- ☐☐ *Alpha video* ☐☐ *www.transformourworld.org*

STEP 9 – *Community*
Pray about your disciples' discipling activities.

TO DO
(Page 36)
- ☐☐ *1 John 1:7* ☐☐ *Alpha video*
- ☐☐ *Read Ekklesia*

STEP 10 – *Disciple!*
Talk about your disciples' discipling.

TO DO
(Page 37)
- ☐☐ *John 14:21*
- ☐☐ *Alpha video*
- ☐☐ *Plan to multiply disciples*

STUDY THE SCRIPTURES BIBLE STUDY

Now that you have finished the **DISCIPLE!** encounters you can strengthen your grip on the Scriptures by doing STS *(Study The Scriptures)* chapter studies.

The STS Bible study is a suggested outline to follow for individual preparation of a Bible study — chapter-by-chapter and week-by-week. Start these after the completion of the *DISCIPLE!* encounter.

We suggest doing these studies in small groups with several of your disciples if possible. Meeting time should be about an hour to an hour and half. Give the leadership of the study to a different person each time you meet. Many have found that beginning this type of study in a short pastoral epistle such as 2 Timothy is good because a short book with short chapters provides comfortable "bite size" portions for getting started. With concentration the preparation can be done in about an hour. The instructions are simple.

1. OUTLINE OR SUMMARY
(Of the assigned chapter for the week).
Some prefer to outline the chapter and others are more at home writing a summary. The summary should be limited to an average of five words per verse. In both cases write the verse numbers in the left-hand margin for easy referencing later in the group study. The back page provides extra space.

2. TITLE
By the time you have finished outlining or summarizing the chapter, you will be able to write your own original title for it.

3. PARALLEL OR CONTRASTING PASSAGES
In this section you are stretched. The object is to find as many cross-references (parallel of contrasting passages) as possible without using margin notes or any kind of study help. Because this is difficult in the beginning, it is best to start by limiting the time spent to 15 minutes. The process of turning the pages of your Bible and searching for something is a great learning process.

4. PROBLEMS
State either real problems (things you do not understand) or potential problems (things that a new Christ follower might not understand). **Write the verse numbers in the left-hand margin.**

5. PERSONAL APPLICATION
This is the single most important part of the STS study and should reflect how the Lord speaks to you personally as you search His Word. It reflects you, your life, your needs, your context, and God's encouragement, direction, comfort, and call to follow Him.

PRAYER REQUESTS
STEP 1 - Following Christ

Prayer requests	Answered prayer	Date

PRAYER REQUESTS
STEP 2 - The basis of being a Disciple

Prayer requests	Answered prayer	Date

PRAYER REQUESTS
STEP 3 - The Wheel

Prayer requests	Answered prayer	Date

PRAYER REQUESTS
STEP 4 - The Lordship of Christ

Prayer requests	Answered prayer	Date

PRAYER REQUESTS
STEP 5 - The Holy Spirit

Prayer requests	Answered prayer	Date

PRAYER REQUESTS
STEP 6 - The Word

Prayer requests	Answered prayer	Date

PRAYER REQUESTS
STEP 7 - Prayer

Prayer requests	Answered prayer	Date

PRAYER REQUESTS
STEP 8 - Witness

Prayer requests	Answered prayer	Date

PRAYER REQUESTS
STEP 9 - Community

Prayer requests	Answered prayer	Date

PRAYER REQUESTS
STEP 10 - Disciple!

Prayer requests	Answered prayer	Date

www.ingramcontent.com/pod-product-compliance
Lightning Source LLC
Chambersburg PA
CBHW071321080526
44587CB00018B/3308